The Good Communicator

The Good Communicator

The eight rules the experts know and never shared.

Nan Kilkeary

Evanston, Illinois

The Good Communicator

Copyright © 1987 by Nan Kilkeary

Library of Congress Cataloging in Publication Data

Kilkeary, Nan, 1943-
    The Good Communicator.
    1. Interpersonal communication.
2. Communication in management.   I. Title.
BF637.C45K5   1987   153.6   86-63734

ISBN 0-942263-08-1

For everyone who has tried to communicate, failed, and didn't know why. This may make it easier.

And especially for Kit and Tim, who always make it clear when I fail to communicate.

Contents

Introduction

The Question   1

The Barrier   7

The Audience Rule   17
   Summary   31

The Sales Rule   33
   Summary   43

The Language Rule   45
   Summary   53

The Repetition Rule   55
   Summary   63

The Challenge Rule   65
   Summary   71

The Truth Rule   73
   Summary   93

The Bad News Rule   95
   Summary   105

The Good News Rule   107
   Summary   113

Good Communicating   115

Introduction

WE DIDN'T communicate. They didn't communicate. I didn't. You didn't. He-she-it didn't.

And we lost our jobs. Our promotions. Our raises. Our chance to attack a new challenge. We lost our income, our investments, financial opportunities.

And we lost our friends, our children, our spouses, our relationships with trusted associates.

All because we couldn't say what we really wanted to say, or didn't see the need to say anything at all, or tried to cover up bad news, or forgot who we were talking to.

Like many of the good things in life, Good Communication is simple.

Of course, that doesn't mean that it's *easy*. It's actually fairly difficult, given the fact that most of us grow up predisposed to believe that whatever we have to say must be critically important—and right—because it falls off our own golden tongues.

Everyone communicates. Some of us are good at it, some of us are bad. But we all do it...with our words, with our bodies, with our memos and letters and reports, with the words we don't speak as well as the ones we do.

Actions frequently speak louder than words—and should be listened to as carefully. But the Good Listener is another book, and what we are concerned about here is words. More specifically, the words you speak as you try to present yourself and your ideas to another person.

This book is based on the assumption that you'd like to be a better communicator if only you knew how. If you're not a good communicator and you know it and you want to continue to hide behind a barrier of misunderstanding, stop reading here.

The simple rules that follow are the essence of good communication. Clearly they are not all there is to know about the subject, but they will give you a fast start. They are distilled from the author's career experience as a professional "communicator" and from the knowledge and experience of countless associates and friends.

These rules are not academic. They are personal, and they are useful. They have been tested over and over again, successfully, by some of America's largest corporations and best executives. They work.

The Question

THE YOUNG man sat dejectedly in the corner chair, watching the coffee softly swirl in a nearly empty cup.

"Where have I gone wrong?" he asked the friend sitting across the table. "What have I *done* wrong?"

"What did they tell you?" his friend asked.

"My boss said..." His voice broke.

"My boss said that my work was good. Whatever I did, I did right. But that it wasn't enough. Someone in my position, someone who supervised other people and who had to deal with all levels of management, had to have other qualities. He said they had to be able to *communicate*, and that I didn't know how.

"And then he fired me. What the devil did he mean, I don't know how to communicate? It's not like I'm antisocial...I talk to people all the time."

He stopped speaking and returned to the view inside his coffee cup.

And then he spoke with a sigh. "The problem is, my wife said the same thing: 'You just don't know how to communicate.' She said she didn't know how I felt, even about her, or what was important to me, or even what I wanted to do. And then she left.

"I never thought of myself as a bad communicator. In fact, I never thought of myself as a communicator at all. Who does? But my life has fallen apart, and the most important people in it are telling me that the problem is not who I am or what I do but how I communicate.

"And I don't even know what they mean.

"Can being a better communicator really make a difference? Can it help me get my job back, help me keep it? Can it help me get promotions? Can it help me get my wife back, help me keep our marriage together?"

"It can make a difference," his friend responded, "especially in today's society, where our ability to market ourselves has become so important. Good communicating isn't a panacea, of course. By itself, it won't get you your job back, nor will it help you get promoted if you can't do the work. It certainly won't save a marriage or even a friendship that doesn't have other substance to it.

"But sometimes it can make a critical difference in a relationship, whether it's with a boss or a subordinate, a wife, husband, parent, child. Yes, I believe it can make a difference."

"How do I change?" the young man asked. "What do I have to learn? Where do I learn it? What makes a good communicator, anyhow? And can I really become one?"

"Anyone can become a good communicator," his friend answered. "It's really a question of learning *how*."

"Where can I learn?" the young man asked.

"I think I know someone who can help you," his friend answered. "Like you, he was troubled early in life with an inability to communicate well. But he studied how the best communicators work, and now he's known to both his colleagues and his friends as a Good Communicator. Here's his phone number," she said, handing the young man a slip of paper.

"I'll call him tomorrow," the young man said. "Will he talk to me?"

"Oh, I think so," his friend answered. "Like everyone else who has studied a subject in depth and then been able to apply the knowledge well, he likes to talk about it. He likes to *communicate*, especially about communicating. I think he'll be pleased to get your call."

The Barrier

THE YOUNG man was greeted at the office door by an older executive, who extended his hand and said "Welcome" with enthusiasm.

"Please come in," he said. He and the young man entered the office and sat down on a sofa near the window to talk.

"I feel foolish," the young man said. "I'm told that I need to learn to communicate better, and I don't know how. But I really do want to learn—my career and my marriage, both of which are vitally important to me— may depend on it. I'm desperate for help."

"I'd be glad to share what I've learned with you," the Good Communicator said. "But I sincerely doubt that good communications is the answer to your problems, though I admit that those who are skilled communicators often have an easier time of it in both their business and personal relationships.

"Usually," he continued, "I find that people who lack communications skills are avoiding dealing with other problems, and that it is the other problems that are really the issue."

"Like what?" the young man asked.

The older man laughed. "One basic thing, really. One very basic thing. So basic and so simple that most of us have been ignoring it all our lives. And it becomes a major problem by the time we even *think* about it."

"What is it?" the young man asked, with decidedly more urgency.

"Our own egos, our feeling that each of us is the center of the universe, or at least of our own universe," the Good Communicator said, smiling.

"Simple, isn't it? Even elementary.

"Our ego keeps us from recognizing something very important about communicating...that the other person is almost always more interested in themselves and what our message means to them. Of course, we're more interested in ourselves and what our message means to us and what we want the other person to do.

"That wall—that war—between egos is the biggest barrier that was ever built to hamper good communications.

"It makes sense, of course," the Good Communicator continued. "Each of us is truly convinced that the way we look at the world and the information we have to communicate is the true picture of reality. At the very least, it's the most important picture of the world.

"We want to share that picture with the people around us, the people we live with and talk to on the street, the people we work with. We want to convince them that our view of things is the world as it *should* be."

The young man was nodding vigorously in agreement.

"There, you see," the older man said with a gentle smile. "You agree with that. In fact, I can't think of anyone who wouldn't.

"If you thought about it, you'd probably even think that I was communicating rather well, wouldn't you?" he asked.

The young man was smiling, still nodding yes.

"In fact, though I'd like to think that I was speaking clearly, I was hardly communicating at all," the older man continued.

The younger man twisted slightly in his chair.

"The real test of communication is whether or not I can present an idea that you may not agree with, and still have you nodding pleasantly when I've finished, even if you don't share my opinion," he said.

"It's whether or not I can persuade you that my viewpoint—my view of reality—is even worthy of your consideration. And of course, that's where the real trouble starts, and where the real challenge of communicating starts...not in dealing with information or chitchat that all of us agree on, but in dealing with information where we may have substantial differences or disagreements.

"It's not unlike falling in love," he said.

The young man sat up straighter.

The older man just laughed. "In case you didn't know it, you just communicated to me that you're more interested in this subject than the subject of a few minutes ago. Well, let me explain.

"When you fall in love with someone, much of your initial conversation—what we're all inclined to call communication, even with a capital "C"—focuses on shared experiences, likes and dislikes, viewpoints and opinions.

"To say it's easy would be an understatement. It's one of life's great highs.

"It isn't until later in the relationship that the need for *effortful* communication comes into play. That's the point where you discover meaningful differences. Then, because you value the other person so highly, you make a real effort to share your opinions and information carefully.

"You don't want to step on his or her toes, because his or her opinion is vitally important to you.

"And you don't want to present your knowledge in an obtuse manner because you really and truly want your sweetheart to understand. You're not being conde-scending, you're just sharing.

"So you work really hard and with great care to pre-sent yourself or your knowledge to this very special person whose opinion is so important.

"*You forget your own ego and concentrate on your partner's.*"

The young man was concentrating hard. "I remember doing that with my wife," he said. "I did work really hard at sharing with her, and she worked equally hard at sharing with me. We understood each other.

"But then something changed," he said.

"Any number of things could have changed," the older man said. "But one of the things I'm pretty sure changed—because you told me so—was your ability to communicate.

"Probably you stopped making the same effort to communicate. Probably you got back inside your ego—a psychologist would say that your ego boundaries snapped back into place—and you stopped concentrating on her ego, and how to reach it. You assumed that the job of communicating was done because you had done it once, and done it well."

The young man was nodding yes, but not happily.

"At some point, you made a shift—and I'd bet that she did, too—to where you cared less about whether the other person heard what you had to say and more about saying it.

"That was where your ego—your sense of your own importance—took over and got in the way of your *communicating.* "

The young man looked despondent.

"Don't look so grim," the older man said gently. "Most of us are guilty of doing just that. It happens in business all the time, too.

"For example, I can't tell you the number of chief executive officers who have spent hundreds of

thousands of dollars to explain the American economic system to their employees, even to their shareholders. They were convinced no one understood it
because their employees didn't share their perspective.

"What those CEOs were doing was talking, but they
weren't communicating, because they weren't paying
any attention to whether or not the people they were
talking to were interested or persuaded.

"Their egos—their sense of the importance of their
own knowledge and message—got in the way of their
communicating that knowledge.

"The ego barrier is a tough one to break through," he
continued, still smiling. "In fact, as tough as it is in
interpersonal relationships, I think it's even tougher
in business. That's because so many businesspeople
get paid for *telling* someone else what to do or think.
But that's not communicating. When you *reach* the
other person, that's communicating.

"You'll never be able to do that if you can't break the
ego barrier," the Good Communicator said.

The young man looked up from the spot he had been
staring at on his folded hands. "Surely there's more to
being a good communicator than that," he said, with
some anger in his voice.

"Yes, of course there is," the older man said. "There
are a number of techniques...reminders...rules that
seem to apply in most communications situations.
Everyone who becomes a Good Communicator learns
them in one form or another.

"Usually, they've learned to apply or understand the
rules long before they can name them. But it's quite

possible, I think, to learn the rules as a method of becoming a Good Communicator."

"Can I be your student?" the younger man asked earnestly. "I'm told that you really are a Good Communicator, and I'm truly in need of help."

"I'll be glad to talk with you about communicating," the Good Communicator responded. "I always enjoy talking about the subject. But you'll have to be your own teacher, and work on applying the rules on your own. You'll have to get out from behind your ego barrier and pay attention to whether other people are receiving what you say, or whether you're just talking at them. If you'll take the responsibility of paying attention to the reception of your messages, I'll take the time to talk with you further."

"I will, I will. When can we start?" the young man asked.

"Come back later this week," the Good Communicator answered. "Right now, I have to end our discussion. I have a meeting shortly and I want to review the messages I plan to deliver so that I can make the best use of my audience's time.

"I'm looking forward to talking with you later," he said, and stood, shaking hands as the meeting ended. "Don't forget to work on dropping your ego barrier," he said, laughing.

The Audience Rule

"WHEN LAST we met," the Good Communicator said, "we were talking about egos and how they create a barrier to good communication. How do you feel about that barrier today?"

"Well," said the young man, "it does seem to me to be an awfully simple approach. I mean, if we could all get out from behind our egos, wouldn't that solve our communications problems?"

"I do wish it were that simple," the older man said. "But tearing down that wall would certainly take a lot of people in the right direction, which is *towards* the other person. The way many of us communicate is akin to standing behind a wall and lobbing grenades of information at the other person—whom we can't see—and hoping that the grenade makes a direct hit. Since we can't see over the wall, we don't know what will happen.

"Sometimes the other person picks up the grenade and lobs it back.

"We're hardly ever ready for *that*," he said, laughing along with the young man.

"The person on the other side of the wall, on the other side of the ego barrier, is our *audience*. And they're vitally important to us.

"Without an audience, there's no one to listen to our precious words.

"Without an audience, there's no one to respond.

"Without an audience, there's no one to persuade.

"Without an audience, there's no feedback.

"Without an audience, you might as well talk to the mirror. And frankly, a lot of people try to do just that," the Good Communicator said.

"It's the 20th century version of the age-old philosophical riddle: if a tree fell in the forest and there was no one to hear it fall, would there be a sound? In this case, it's 'if the words fall off your tongue and there's no one to hear them, have you spoken?' " he said.

"I'd say that you haven't," he said.

"But what about a situation when the other person has to hear you?" the young man asked. "Let's say I'm talking to a subordinate and that person has to hear what I tell them because I'm their boss?"

"I wouldn't bet for a moment that the fact that the person *must* hear what you say means that they have. What your audience wants to hear is always more important than what you want to tell them. Always.

"Think of dealing with a recalcitrant little boy. You can tell that child forever and ever to pick up his toys. And he won't hear you. But tell him to pick up his toys before you go out for an ice cream cone and you've hooked your audience. It was important for you to talk about the toys, but it was important for him to hear about the ice cream cone."

The younger man looked restless. "But my employees have to listen," he stated. "They get paid to listen to what I say to them. That's their job."

"We're talking about being a Good Communicator," the older man said testily, "not Attila the Hun. An executive, a friend, a parent, a lover who intends to be a Good Communicator can't stop with the fact that their audience has ears.

"You have to find a way to tickle their ears."

"The best way I know of to begin to do that is to put yourself in your audience's mind...the old Indian trick of walking in another man's or woman's moccasins. I don't find that very hard to do when I concentrate on it.

"Let's go back to your employees. Sure they have to listen, but that doesn't mean they're getting the message. And sure, you can say that part of their job is to listen. And it is. But that doesn't mean that they're getting the message you want them to hear. It doesn't mean that you're communicating.

"You can't count on your audience to hear what you want to say, although surely in an ideal world they would. *You have to count on yourself to say what they want to hear.*

"That means getting out of your ego—out from behind the barriers—and figuring out what it is they actually want to hear. What would your staff want to hear?" The Good Communicator asked.

"They'd probably like to hear they'd done a good job," the young man said.

"Of course," the older man said, "we all would. "

"And they'd like to know what kinds of opportunities they had, and whether I thought they could succeed."

"Go on," the older man said.

"I think they'd like to know how valuable their work is and how it fits into the organization...and what's going on in the company that affects their work...I always want to know those things myself," the young man said.

"Precisely!" said the Good Communicator. "When you begin to think of what you'd like to hear from someone in your position, whatever that position is, then you're beginning to think from the minds of the audience. You're beginning to understand the importance of what they want to hear.

"Your audience can't hear you, won't hear you, if what you say isn't important to them. Oh, it can be important for lots of reasons, and some of them may even be quite silly, but your information must have *value* to the people receiving it. Think of some examples...

...getting something free.

...getting a pat on the back.

...getting feedback or criticism you can accept that will

help you make changes so that you can reach your goals.

...learning that someone thinks you're unique, or learning ways that you are unique.

...getting information you need to do your job better.

...getting more information about a favorite activity or hobby or interest.

...learning more about solving the problems in your life.

...getting information that will help you make money.

...good gossip.

...sharing a secret, feeling valued because not very many people know what you know.

...being entertained or amused.

"One of the keys of reaching your audience is figuring out what has value to them and how to present what you want to say in terms of that value. Unless you can make that jump, the chances are pretty high that you'll only be delivering part of your message—no matter what kind of captive audience you have—because you won't be operating in the same framework."

"But doesn't the audience have some responsibility for hearing?" the young man asked plaintively.

"It would be nice if they did," the Good Communicator said. "Yes, it certainly would be nice. But I can't think of too many instances where the responsibility of the audience to hear is as high as the responsibility of the speaker to reach them.

"After all, in 999 out of a thousand times, the speaker is the one who benefits if the listener understands. I suppose you could make exceptions for instances where the audience is about to be exposed to life-threatening danger and saving their lives is infinitely more important to them than it is to the speaker. In that kind of a situation, I'd say that the audience is willing to take total responsibility for hearing," the older man laughed.

"If you're an executive talking to a journalist," he continued, "the journalist has some professional and ethical reasons for listening. After all, he or she is a paid listener and observer. But even in that case, the reporter will have other things on his or her mind, and will bring other perspectives and goals even to listening. Reporters, for example, are likely to be listening for a headline in your statements, because a good headline and the byline that goes with it are the recognition they earn.

"In the real world, of course, many people are interested in what you have to say...at least at first," the Good Communicator continued.

"But if you want to be a Good Communicator, you'd better assume that what they want to hear is infinitely more important to them than what you want to say. That's always a safe assumption, and it puts the burden of communicating where it belongs...on you. After all, you're the one with the message to deliver, aren't you? And you're the one who gains the most if the message is understood...even more if it's understood and *accepted*."

The young man was clearly uncomfortable, squirming in his chair.

"'I can see that you don't like this idea," the Good Communicator said.

The young man nodded his agreement without looking up.

"I can see that you'd prefer that the audience take more of the responsibility."

The older man sighed.

"Let's go back a step," he said. "When we first talked, you told me that becoming a Good Communicator was important to you because being a bad communicator had cost you your job and your marriage, the very things that you said made your life worthwhile."

The young man nodded again.

"Surely," the older man said gently, patting the younger on the knee, "you didn't think that you could become a Good Communicator by giving the responsibility to the people who complained in the first place?"

The young man looked up, startled.

"Being a Good Communicator is hard work, no doubt," the older man said. "If it were easy, more of us would be good at it, wouldn't we? And those people who are important to us wouldn't be complaining about our inability to communicate.

"Of course," the older man said, laughing gently, "you do understand that when people tell us we aren't communicating, what they're really saying is that we're not telling them what they want to hear?"

The younger man laughed, too.

"Is that what my wife means?" he asked. "Is that what my boss means? Just that I'm not telling them what they want to hear?"

"I'm sure that's a good part of it," the older man said. "That isn't all there is to Good Communicating, of course, but it will help you understand that what the audience wants to hear—even *can* hear—is infinitely more important than what you want to say. Maybe it will even help you walk in their shoes, a little."

"But how do I get across what I want to say?" the younger man asked.

"No matter how well you speak or structure your message—and many people are truly ingenious at packaging their messages—you won't be able to truly communicate until you understand the significance of the audience," the Good Communicator said.

"You won't be able to truly communicate until you recognize that what you have to say may be irrelevant to your most important audiences, and that it's your responsibility to find a way to make your words heard by making them relevant to the other person," he continued.

"Let's talk about an easy example," the older man said.

"Suppose you're a senior level corporate executive, something you obviously aspire to be. Here's a problem that companies face all the time...your company has just had a year in which profits are not as high as predicted because growth in your industry has slowed down.

"An insensitive executive, in talking about the down-turn, would focus on problems in the industry. It wouldn't be wrong, of course, because that's where the problem is. You'd probably agree that he'd sound like he was passing the responsibility."

The young man nodded his agreement.

"In fact, he might not be. He might just be defining the problem accurately," the older man said. "But that probably isn't what his separate audiences care about. It isn't what's most relevant to them.

"A Good Communicator would address each concerned audience only after thinking about *their* worries.

"He or she would talk to shareholders about their investment concerns, about whether the price of the stock was holding up, about the continuation of the dividend policy, about the long-term quality of their investments.

"He'd talk to his fellow executives about what the company needed to do to respond to industry trends, reacting to their concerns about the future of the business.

"He'd talk to employees about needed actions to keep the company growing, and how that impacted their jobs. Certainly, he'd recognize that their first concern would be their jobs, and he'd reassure them on that point first if he could.

"And he would go home at night and talk with his spouse about the security of his own employment, what changes he could expect in his own working environment, and what impact he expected that to have on the family.

"In every case he would be making his message relevant to his audience by recognizing their concerns and addressing them. His spouse may listen to him complain about the industry reversals, but what she cares about is the impact on her own life.

"Makes sense, doesn't it?" the Good Communicator asked.

"I have to admit that it does," the young man replied. "But what do you do when the audience just doesn't get the message, no matter how hard you try?"

"We haven't talked about whether or not your audience believes what you have to say," the older man said. "Nor have we talked about whether they agree with it. Those, I think, are topics for other meetings.

"I think your question has to do with what to do to get through to all of those people when you're really trying to tell them something—when you're taking the responsibility for communicating—and they're not hearing you?" he asked quizzically.

The young man nodded again.

"My experience has been universally that when an audience isn't getting the message...and this is a question of not hearing it, not an issue of not agreeing with it...that the problem is the *message*.

"Not the audience...those dummies," he said with mock scorn.

"Not the delivery system, whatever it may be...a personal conversation, a speech, a printed article, a video program, an ad. Delivery systems, of course, have an impact, but they can't carry the message by themselves. I'd even go so far as to say that if your advertising isn't delivering, maybe you don't have anything to advertise. But that has to do with the truth and substance of the message, and that too is a subject for another day.

"When the message isn't getting through, believe me, the problem is the message.

"It's the expectation of the speaker that once the audience hears what she has to say, they will automatically accept her point of view.

"It's forgetting to make the message valuable to the audience.

"It's the speaker barricading himself behind his ego barrier and lobbing information grenades."

The young man sighed deeply.

"I must admit that I'm getting discouraged," he said. "It's much easier to just tell the other person, or the other people, what you want to tell them. I've always learned that if I just said things clearly, if I just told people what I wanted or what I knew clearly, that I'd done the job.

"Now you're telling me that I can't be a Good Communicator by doing that. You're telling me that I have to giftwrap what I have to say so that the other person will want to unwrap the box."

"That's a pretty good description," the older man said. "Yes, I'd say you really communicated with that description. I think it's very accurate in many ways. It certainly gets at the problem of the unacceptability of the message. Nice work."

The young man smiled for the first time in the meeting.

"OK," he said. "I'm beginning to get it. I guess you've even known all along that what you had to say was interesting, even essential, to me. Frankly, I'd rather leave the burden on the audience's shoulders. It's much easier."

"It is, it is," the older man agreed. "But it isn't Good Communicating."

"What happens," the young man asked, "when my audience might not want to hear something, but I think it's really important, even vitally important, that they should?"

"If it's that important to your audience, I'm sure they'll want to listen, especially if you've thought through what parts of it are valuable to them. Even bad news can be enormously important and can command attention," the Good Communicator responded.

"But what if it's something I think they really need to hear but the audience doesn't see the value of it?" the younger man pressed.

"It seems to me," the Good Communicator continued, "that if you've gone to the effort to make the information valuable to them...even interesting...and your audience still doesn't care, if you still can't interest them, then you ought to stop trying."

The young man groaned.

"I see," the older man said, "that you're still struggling with the reality that there are people who don't want to hear what you have to say, regardless of how important you think it is.

"That really is frustrating. Of course, you can try harder to make the message interesting, and many times paying more attention to what the audience wants to hear will help you make your message more acceptable. But sometimes it won't.

"Sometimes no one wants to hear what you have to say, under any circumstances.

"Let me talk about a couple of absolute examples. Suppose you tell your spouse, who wants to remain married, that you want a divorce. Nothing you can do, no amount of effort, can make that message acceptable to your audience. The very best you can hope to do is present it in a form that will make it understandable. Under those circumstances, I think even that's asking a lot.

"Put the same sort of situation into a business environment. Suppose you have to fire an employee of long standing with the company, an employee who's never worked anywhere else. Let's assume that the firing is unquestionably necessary. Would you expect the employee to find your message acceptable?   Of course not. You'd be relieved if he even understood it.

"Now let's try something a little less absolute. You're at home trying to explain to your six-year-old daughter why she should develop good savings habits and put a dime of her 50 cent allowance into her piggy bank each week. But she knows that her favorite treat, a chocolate fudge ice cream cone, costs 43 cents, including tax. I can't imagine the two of you ever understanding each other, unless you can provide her with a bigger incentive than her weekly chocolate fudge ice cream...and perhaps you can think of one. But the reality is that your message isn't getting through as long as visions of chocolate fudge ice cream are dancing in her head.

"If your audience doesn't think what you have to say is important and if you can't find a way to make it more attractive—if the chocolate fudge is getting in the way—it still doesn't matter how important you think your message is.

"That's why the audience is so critically important," the Good Communicator said. "That's why none of us can be Good Communicators until we can remember the audience is more important than the message.

"Without the audience, there is no message."

The Audience Rule:

Tickle their ears.

• Put yourself in your audience's mind.

• What the audience wants to hear is more important than what you want to tell them. Always.

• The audience won't listen unless what you have to say has value to them. Determine that value.

• It's the responsibility of the speaker to reach the audience, not the responsibility of the audience to hear.

• What's important to you may be irrelevant to your audience.

• When your audience isn't responding, the problem is usually the message and its acceptability, not the delivery system or the audience.

• If you're convinced that your audience should listen because what you have to say is important, find a way to convince them, or forget it.

The Sales Rule

"I'VE BEEN thinking about reaching my audience," the young man said at their next meeting. "I recognize that I have to make more of an effort to reach the audience, rather than just expecting that they will listen because I have something I want to say.

"And I recognize that I have to think in terms of the value my words have to the audience. That's a difficult transition to make," he continued.

"It is difficult," the older man said. "Many, many people are never able to do it. Many people who could be Good Communicators never get there because they still want to put the responsibility on their audience. But Good Communicating doesn't work that way."

"I've already started to apply it," the young man said. "When I interview for a job, I think in terms of what the interviewer needs to know...how I might fit into her organization...how the company could benefit from my skills...rather than just talking about how good I am at my profession.

"It's amazing, but my interviews are going much more positively," he said.

"Not so amazing," the Good Communicator said. "You've begun to think in terms of what has value to your audience. It doesn't surprise me that your audience responds more positively."

"But I still can't get past the idea," the young man said, "that the audience should be interested in what I have to say, especially if it's something that could be useful to them."

"Let's assume that you have a product that could be useful to your client, but that he doesn't know it," the older man said. "How would you go about bringing the two together?"

"Why, I'd try to sell him on the benefits of the product," the young man said.

"Of course you would. Anybody with any brains would. You know your client—your audience—and his needs, and you know the product and its benefits. What you'd try to do is outline those benefits to the client so that he perceives the value.

"If you do a good job of it...if your client trusts you and the benefits of the product are clear...you'll probably end up making a sale, and you'll both benefit."

"Is that what we're talking about?" the young man asked. "Selling? Are you saying that's all I have to do...sell?"

"Good Communication is based on good selling, no question about it," the older man said. "Still, it isn't quite that simple.

"Good selling, of course, is based on the essential respect that the salesperson has for his customer. And that's a good part of what we were talking about in our conversations about the audience. When you think in terms of selling, you begin to think in terms of making an effort to reach the other person.

"It's the next step beyond considering your audience and their viewpoint. It's making an *active* effort to reach them, to take your message to them, as well as recognizing what value that message may have.

"It is not only walking in other peoples' shoes, but also meeting them on the path and helping them select and fit the shoes—the shoes they want—in the first place."

"And, of course, the shoes come in all sizes and colors," the older man continued.

"Oh," said the young man suddenly. "If Good Communication is good selling, then I can use that to sell any number of things...products, ideas, programs."

"Even yourself," said the Good Communicator. "Even yourself. Which, of course, is what you do all the time, even when you're not conscious of it.

"When you are conscious of it...say, when you're trying to impress a new acquaintance...you're very careful of how you sell yourself. Your appearance, your mannerisms, your words, are all part of your sales package.

"Your goal as a Good Communicator should be to become more conscious of how you sell yourself and your ideas, your products, more of the time."

"Let me see if I've got it," the young man said. "If I have something I want to communicate, I should think of it in terms of selling to my audience, persuading them that what I have to offer has value to them."

"Another way to think of it is goal-oriented communication," the older man said.

"When you approach an interaction, think through what has value to your audience—where they're coming from—and then rehearse presenting yourself or your product or your idea within their framework.

"Most of the time, we don't go through the goal-setting phase, nor the rehearsal. And much of the time, it may be unnecessary because we know what to do and say in a given situation instinctively. But if you're having trouble communicating or you're approaching a difficult audience, it's an important step to take."

"Are you saying that you rehearse everything you want to say before you meet with someone?" the younger man asked.

"No, no. Many—most—of our interactions are natural to us. There is, after all, a reason for etiquette, for good manners. It gets us through most social situations," the older man said.

"But I do rehearse...and so do other Good Communicators...when the outcome of a particular meeting is important to me. Novices at communication do this naturally. Remember rehearsing your conversation for your first date when you were a teenager? Or rehearsing for your first job interview? Or asking for your first raise? Rehearsal was natural to you then because the whole process was new.

"Good Communicators never stop rehearsing, because the outcome is still important to them. You'll recall that I had to close our first meeting because I needed time to mentally rehearse for an important meeting."

"You're still rehearsing, even with all your experience?" the young man asked incredulously.

"It does get easier," the older man answered. "But yes, I still rehearse for important situations. I'd be foolish to throw away the opportunity for greater success that comes from defining my important messages and thinking through the concerns of my audience and how to sell them my message.

"And there are some situations that always call for rehearsal...interviews where you're likely to be quoted...speeches...other presentations where what you say and how you say it become matters of public record. Why blow the sale?"

"If Good Communicating is good selling," the young man said, "then your goal is closing the sale, isn't it?"

"Of course," said the older man. "When you want to have an impact on someone, you want them to buy what you are selling, even if what you're selling is yourself. So of course, after you've presented your pitch, after you've listened to their response and responded to their concerns, you want to close the sale...get their agreement."

"What happens," the young man asked, "when the other person just isn't buying? When they just don't agree?"

"Even the best communicators don't win all the time...can't always close the sale," the older man said. "When that happens, you have to question whether there's anything else you could have done. Did you know and consider the audience's concerns? Did your information have value to them? Were you talking to yourself or the other person? Was your goal clear, and did you prepare adequately?

"Sometimes the other fellow just isn't in the market for your product.

"You may not be able to sell your idea, your product, yourself—and not being able to sell yourself is the most painful rejection—but I'd say that if the other person accepts the validity of your message, you've succeeded...even though you didn't reach your goal.

"Let's talk about a business situation. You're an executive whose small-town factory is being closed because of product obsolescence and declining sales. You're talking to the editor of the local newspaper, who is outraged by the loss of jobs, and frightened by the potential loss of circulation. You've presented facts and figures that led to the decision, which was painful for you and your management team. You've said that. You've told the editor how long it took to make the decision and how many people were involved. You've explained what your company will do to help employees find other work, and what your severance policy is.

"But no amount of well-planned communication is ever going to persuade that editor, who also has an audience to answer to, that you've made the right decision.

"In that situation, getting the editor to accept the *validity* of your position is a very positive accomplishment. It's probably the most positive response you could achieve.

"There are certainly many times when getting the other person just to accept our right to our viewpoint and our decision is a major achievement."

"I can think of personal situations where that would apply," the young man said. "Getting someone of another religion to accept mine would be difficult. But I could convince them that my viewpoint was well considered, too."

"A good example," said the older man. "There are many times when your communications goal can only be peaceful co-existence, when you can't 'close the sale,' because the other person can't reasonably accept your viewpoint.

"In fact, in situations like that," the Good Communicator continued, "I'd say it was Bad Communicating to try to impose your thinking on the other person.

"You'd be disregarding everything we've talked about so far. You'd be staying behind your ego barrier, assuming that your viewpoint is more valuable. You'd have forgotten to consider the audience's concerns and values. Forgotten to rehearse your presentation to answer their concerns.

"But most of all, you'd have shown that you didn't respect your audience and what they brought to the interaction.

"You'd have forgotten to *sell*. It's a fatal mistake."

The Sales Rule:

Good Communication is good selling.

• Good communication is the effort of one person to sell another person on an idea, program, concept, behavior, viewpoint, product. . .even the person himself.

• Good Communication has a goal. The Good Communicator acknowledges and defines his goal and shapes his words to help achieve it.

• Good Communications should be rehearsed.

• The Good Communicator recognizes that he is succeeding in communicating when his audience has accepted the validity of his viewpoint.

• Bad Communication is the attempt of one person to *impose* a product, idea or viewpoint on another person without having first determined the value of the time to the receiver.

The Language Rule

"YOU KNOW," the Good Communicator continued, "I think this would be a good time to talk about words."

"Words?" asked the young man. "I thought that's what we were talking about all along."

"So we have," the older man said. "We've been talking about how to reach the other person—or people—with words, not what the words themselves are.

"The words themselves become important, too."

"You mean that if I select my words carefully, even artfully, I can be more persuasive with my audience?" the young man asked.

"Well, yes," the older man responded. "But frankly, I was thinking more of words as barriers.

"Not many of us are statesmen or diplomats or orators with speaking skills so wonderful that our words and phrases are going to end up in a reference book. No, leave the gold-plated phrases to speechwriters unless you happen to have a natural talent for it, and not many of us do. I know I don't.

"What I'm talking about is the way we use words to *keep* from reaching our audience," he continued.

"Think about it," he said. "The first thing on our minds when we're speaking with or to someone is impressing the other person. And the first thing we tend to do with our words is tie them up in knots to show the other person how complex our mind is, to impress them with how wonderful we are."

"I do admit that the first thing on my ego is impressing the other person," the younger man said.

"I think we'd both agree that a desire to impress someone new—whatever we want that impression to be—is part of human nature. It's certainly part of mine," the Good Communicator said.

"Even after working at it for years, my first temptation is to say something impressive and complex," he said. "I still need to remind myself that my goal is to reach the other person, to communicate something about myself or my knowledge and to have them accept it...not that I can be a pompous bore and use fancy words and sentence structure.

"I have to remember that the more convoluted my language becomes, the harder it is for the other person to understand what my message is."

The young man was nodding vigorously.

"I always have trouble with people who use lots of technical jargon," he said. "Sometimes I think they don't want me to understand what they're talking about...that what they're trying to do is keep all their knowledge to themselves so that they can continue to be experts and be superior.

"And it seems to me that people in every business and profession do that," he said.

"You're absolutely right," the older man said. "People in every business do that. Sometimes, they're even hiding the fact that they don't know what they're talking about. Of course, when two people in the same profession are speaking to each other, jargon is perfectly appropriate and necessary. It's a kind of shorthand and everyone knows the code.

"But outside of professional circles, the strongest thing it says is that the speaker wants to stay one-up on the listener, or really doesn't want to communicate. It's a barrier to understanding.

"So are the long convoluted sentences that people put together to try to demonstrate their own intelligence. This happens less often in conversation or spoken language than it does with written language. Think about it."

The younger man adjusted his chair.

"I think I see what you mean," he said. "Textbooks, for example. Sometimes I think that the last thing in the world the authors want to do is educate people by making their subject easy to learn. And the first thing they want to do is show how much they know and how complicated it is.

"I have problems with many textbooks, too," the older man said. "The long sentences are sometimes difficult for me to break up into brain-sized pieces. Shorter sentences may not seem as intellectual, but they do tend to communicate better.

"Short, precise sentences are critically important in speaking, far more important than in writing," he continued. "I can make a strong case for more direct communication with the written word, but directness and precision are absolutely critical with the spoken word."

"Why is it so much more important with the spoken word?" the young man asked.

"Simple," the Good Communicator responded. "You can't reread the spoken word. Unless you've video-taped a newscast, you can't go back and check the reporter's words. You can't rerun a speaker's speech. If you tune out your son's comments on why he needs the car Saturday night, he can't be rewound and replayed.

"When you're saying something out loud, you only get one chance to have your message heard and understood.

"The spoken language is different than the written language," he continued. "What you say out loud disappears and remains only in the memory of you and your audience...and your memories may disagree. You have to be especially careful because your audience can't reread your words.

"They also can't digest huge clumps of words, in deeply convoluted sentences. Their ears just don't work that fast...do yours?"

"Now that I think about it, no," the young man said. "When I'm listening to someone I'm aware of wanting his or her words to be very straightforward so that I don't have to work too hard to understand. It isn't so difficult with printed material because I can pace myself."

"Listening is harder work...a harder way to get substantive information. That's why it's important not to overload your listeners by trying to deliver too much information at one time.

"You have to give them a little breathing room to sort things out. Communicators who want to be sure that the audience is getting their message don't try to overload the circuits by presenting too many messages at one time.

"What they do," the Good Communicator said, "is identify their most important message and make sure that it gets through. It becomes their Primary Communications Objective, and they concentrate on presenting it well, in different forms, and frequently."

"But what about the other messages?" the young man asked.

"Most of us aren't capable of dealing with multiple ideas at one time," the older man said. "Good Communicators know that.

"They know that it's far more important to present their Primary Communications Objective and have it be heard through all the background noise than to present 10 messages that get so garbled in the listener's mind that none come through clearly.

"They know that most people only remember one or two facts or concepts from a conversation or speech, and they work to make sure that what their audience remembers is what they want them to remember... their most important message.

"They know that the first rule of language is always: Keep it simple. And they follow it."

The Language Rule:

Keep it simple.

• The more convoluted your language, the less chance there is that your message will be received.

• Jargon is designed to keep people from understanding you (for professionals, it's shorthand. Outside professional circles, it's patronizing).

• Short sentences say more, more easily, than long sentences.

• Listeners can't rerun or reread your words. Make the message clear the first time. You generally don't get a second chance.

• The more messages you try to deliver at one time, the less chance there is that your important message will be received.

The Repetition Rule

"WELL," the older man said with a smile, "am I making this simple enough? Has following the language rule been easy for you since we last met?"

"I do tend to forget it sometimes," the younger man allowed. "Particularly when I want to impress some-one...then I'm inclined to try to make my words more, well, upscale."

"Perhaps that's because I was concentrating so hard on keeping it simple that I didn't put enough emphasis on the Repetition Rule," the Good Communicator said. "Perhaps I didn't repeat my messages enough to really have them sink in."

"Or perhaps I had other things on my mind and hadn't quite incorporated what I had learned," the young man said with a grin. "But I heard the hook. What's the Repetition Rule?"

"We live in an age of information overload," the older man said. "There are estimates that, even with-out trying, most of us receive thousands and thou-sands of messages a day. We get them from advertise-ments, news bulletins, even disk jockey comments on the radio. We get them from billboards and bus cards on our way to work, even from license plates.

"We get memos and letters and instructions and telephone calls and meetings at work, conversations with our coworkers. We get thousands of messages from the magazines and newspapers we read, countless more from television or whatever other kind of entertainment we choose.

"You can't even go to a baseball game without being bombarded with advertising messages on the wall and the scoreboards and in the program and sometimes even on the players as well.

"Business is very busy making sure that we get the product message. But that's part of the fun of it, too. The point is, there are thousands of people out there who want to tell us something and who are vying for our attention.

"Some of them have more important things to say than others, of course," the older man continued. "And by virtue of who they are, some people have a stronger claim on our ears than others. I'm always careful to listen to any message my boss cares to deliver, or anything my family or friends have to say. The people who are important to me have a priority channel."

"But what about the people who don't have a priority channel?" the younger man asked.

"That's the problem," the older man said. "How *do* you get through all those other messages when you don't have a priority channel? How do you make your message heard through the thousands of others that are competing for brain time from your audience?

"Messages that are delivered only once just don't get through that jumble," the Good Communicator said.

"That's why the Repetition Rule is simply "Once is Not Enough."

"If you have a message you want to be heard, you need to deliver it more than one time," he said. "Messages we hear only once don't get through the clutter and stick.

"And that's what you want your message to do...stick. When we were talking about keeping language simple and easy to digest, I mentioned that one of the reasons for that is that verbal—conversational—language can't be reread or rerun. You either get it the first time or you don't.

"And whether or not your audience gets it the first time depends on lots of factors out of your control... like whether it's the first day of spring, how hot the coffee was in the morning, how many phone calls came through, whether the sale was closed or how bad traffic is supposed to be on the way home.

"Unless your audience is truly captive and is vitally interested in the subject, the odds are your message— your Primary Communications Objective—isn't going to stick the first time because it has so much competition from other messages and problems.

"That's one of the reasons to focus on a Primary Communications Objective," the Good Communicator continued. "If you can't be sure that your primary message gets through, why should you even bother about secondary or tertiary messages? No, focus on your Primary Communications Objective.

"And then repeat it and repeat it and repeat it, in as many different forms as you can think of. Any statement worth making is worth making twice. And any statement worth making twice is worth making more than twice."

"I can understand the need, even the necessity, of making statements more than once to make sure they stick," the young man said. "I suppose even a second grader could understand that. But what I don't understand is how to make the statement in different forms. What are you talking about?"

"If you were a senior executive," the older man said, "and you wanted to convince your company's employees that you were putting a new emphasis on customer service, how would you do it?"

"I''d call them all together and talk to as many as I could," the young man said.

"Then what?" asked the older man.

"Well, I guess I'd ask the company newsletter to do an article on my speech and the program," the younger man answered. "Even I can think of that much. But then what?"

"Let me give you some possibilities," the older man said. "How about a videotape on customer service? Then there's notes on the bulletin board...a customer service awards program...a customer complaint column in the newsletter so that employees recognize customer problems...meetings with small groups of employees...training programs on how to deal with customers better.

"All of those things would deliver your Primary Communications Objective, which is to tell employees that there's a new emphasis on customer service. Some of those methods will even help employees actually provide better customer service.

"But then you will have delivered your message in many different ways and forms. I assume, of course, that you'll repeat it over and over in conversations and meetings with peers and employees.

"In a company, you know you've been successful in delivering your Primary Communications Objective when you start hearing other people repeat it. But even then, you must keep the momentum going by continuing to deliver the message."

"Is the same thing true for personal relationships?" the young man asked. "Can you deliver a message a lot of different ways? How?"

"We don't have as many vehicles available to us in personal relationships," the older man said, "or at least we think we don't. But I think they're really there.

"Let's say you were trying to convince your family that moving to another city was a wonderful idea. First, you'd tell them what you thought, and you'd put yourself in their shoes and anticipate their questions—though we'll cover that more when we get to the Challenge Rule.

"Then, in many conversations, you'd repeat your Primary Communications Objective—that moving to Smithville was a plan with many benefits.

"You might get pictures of Smithville and post them on the refrigerator. Or find a videotape from the

Chamber of Commerce and play it on the VCR. You'd search for newsclips of interesting things in Smithville, or statistics that demonstrated the city's benefits.

"And eventually, you'd know that you'd succeeded in communicating your Primary Communications Objective when your family started actively talking about the benefits of Smithville.

"Yes, the Repetition Rule is important for interpersonal relations, too. It just takes a little more imagination to find ways to deliver the message repetitively.

"Most of us are very smart people, but our minds are working so fast on so many things and so many messages are competing for our attention, that we must hear something more than once before we truly recall it," the Good Communicator said. "Once is truly not enough."

The Repetition Rule:

Once is not enough.

• We live in an age of information overload. Messages we hear only once don't get through.

• Verbal messages are especially hard to recall, and the listener can't go back and re-hear them. To make sure they stick, they must be repeated so that the listener knows how important they are.

• Any statement worth making is worth making twice.

• Any statement worth making twice is worth making more than twice.

• Make your statement in as many different ways as possible, but keep making it.

• Despite the fact that most of us are very smart people, we tend not to remember things unless we hear them several times.

The Challenge Rule

"I'M HAVING trouble 'closing the sale,'" the young man said. "Here I am, thinking through what I want to say, thinking about how to make it valuable to my audience, thinking about persuasive selling, and when I get done delivering my message—say, in a job interview—the other person levels a question or contradiction at me and I don't know what to do with it."

"I guess that brings us to the Challenge Rule," the Good Communicator laughed. "So here it is: Do It Yourself."

"What?" the young man asked, perplexed.

"Challenge yourself," the older man said. "The concept is quite simple. It's so simple, in fact, that I'm astounded more people don't use it instinctively. But they don't.

"When you are trying to sell your audience on a concept, anticipate what they are going to ask you about it. Consider where they're going to be negative, and why—which ought not to be too difficult to figure out if you've thought through who they are.

"I assume that you know your subject, or you wouldn't be trying to persuade someone else to accept your point of view. When you know the subject, you know better than anyone else possibly could what the questions about it could be. Ask them...and answer them...even before you get around to delivering your message," the Good Communicator said.

"You mean rehearse questions? And answers?" the young man asked.

"Yes. I told you it was simple. Yet I'm astounded at how few people ever go through this process. I wouldn't think of making a presentation and not challenging myself. If I can't answer the questions in a neutral environment like my own office, how can I possibly hope to answer them in a tense environment like a meeting or interview?

"For a really important situation like trying to sell my boss on a new program, I'll even have my staff sit with me and challenge my presentation, just so that I can get more questions and a more aggressive rehearsal environment.

"There's really no excuse for having a question catch you off-guard if you've done your homework. Watch the President at a news conference. There's hardly ever a question that surprises him or that he isn't ready for. That's because he makes the effort to collect information and rehearse in advance.

"To do otherwise would be just plain stupid," the Good Communicator said.

"Delivering the message is only half the communications process. Answering the questions is the other half. Your job interviews are particularly important to you now. Would you go into an actual interview without rehearsing for challenges?"

"The fact is, I have," the young man said ruefully. "Sure, I think about what I want to say. But I've always assumed that I'd have to wait for another person's questions before thinking about the answers.

"I can see now how limiting that is. I could do a wonderful job presenting myself and then look like a bumbling idiot answering a question I didn't anticipate. I could be throwing away all my original effort by not being ready for questions."

"Absolutely true," the older man said. "Now, which has more credibility, the statement or the answers?"

The young man sat thoughtfully.

"When I'm on the questioning side, I guess the answers to the questions I ask have far more credibility than the original statements.

"I guess that's because I don't expect the speaker to follow the Challenge Rule," he chuckled. "I assume that my question is new and fresh and wonderful and that the answer the speaker gives is, too.

"Answers always *feel* more honest to me than statements, though," the young man said. "Maybe that's because I'm part of the process then...I'm involved in it."

"A good part of the reason that answers to your questions feel more honest to you is exactly that involvement," the older man said. "All of us assume that two-way communication has more integrity than one-way communication, a statement that gets us right back to our audience rule.

"Our involvement with the other person in an exchange of information gives credibility that can never be matched in a one-way process.

"If credibility is part of your goal—and for many public figures credibility is infinitely more important than information—then answers are more important than statements."

"They deserve the same preparations, don't you think?" the Good Communicator asked.

"I"m becoming convinced," the young man said. "Preparing well for challenges also gives me the opportunity to incorporate more information for my audience than I might have been able to use in delivering the original messages."

"That's partly because you have more data about your audience," the older man said. "Once they start asking questions, you have a much better idea of their knowledge and concerns..."

"And I can respond to the needs of the audience while delivering my own message," the young man said, triumphantly.

The Good Communicator laughed.

"I can see that thinking about your audience and their needs is getting to be second nature for you, even in answering questions.

"That's a good thing, because all the same rules apply to questions that apply to the original message. Answers are another way to sell your message to your audience.

"Since they involve the interests of the audience and can increase your credibility, challenges are an especially golden opportunity to communicate.

"Responding to a challenge without preparation," the Good Communicator said, "is a sinful waste of opportunity."

The Challenge Rule:

Do it yourself.

• You know more of the questions that can be asked of you and your story than anyone else. Ask them, and answer them, in advance.

• Any communicator who has prepared the initial information and has ignored questions and challenges has done less than half the job. Devote as much time to the potential challenges as you do to statements.

• Your answers to questions have more credibility than the statements you make because your audience is involved in the process.

• Questions are your opportunity to advance your cause with additional information and with additional credibility.

• Questions are your opportunity to determine the real interests and attitudes of your audience.

• The same communications rules apply to challenges and questions as apply to the original statement.

The Truth Rule

"THE CHALLENGE Rule is an easy one," the Good Communicator continued. "Like the Language Rule or the Repetition Rule, it's something you can use all the time. It's a method, a technique, a tool. It doesn't have anything to do with what you think, or what you think of your audience. It's simply a way to approach an interaction.

"We've talked before about putting yourself in your audience's shoes and presenting your message in terms of the needs of the audience. The Challenge Rule helps you do that by helping you anticipate what your audience is really concerned about.

"If you use the process well, it will help you uncover weaknesses in your own presentation...or your knowledge...or even programs and theories.

"It will help you and your audience uncover the truth," he said.

The young man looked dismayed.

"The truth?" he asked.

"What does the truth have to do with answering my listener's questions? I thought we were talking about techniques, not morality," he snapped.

"So we are, so we are," the older man responded.

"Then why should I worry about truth if I can success-fully answer questions?" the young man asked. "It just doesn't seem relevant to me."

"We're still talking about practical value," the Good Communicator said. "And the truth has practical and relevant value to you, as a communicator."

"Well, I think there are many times when the truth would hurt the people I'm talking to," the younger man said. "And there are certainly times when leaving out information wouldn't hurt anyone."

"I can think of many instances when you're right," the Good Communicator said. "Little white lies, for example, are a perfect case. Or holding your tongue and not giving a truthful opinion when you're in a no-win situation. But we're still talking here about the practical value of truth as a communications technique...and it has enormous value.

"In fact," he said, "I would go so far as to say that it has critical value as a communications technique. You simply can't be a Good Communicator without the truth, any more than you can be a Good Communicator without remembering the audience."

"But I think there are times when the truth is irrelevant or frightening," the young man said. "And there are certainly times when the truth would hurt *me*, and I want to protect myself."

"Well, that's certainly a natural impulse," the older man laughed. "Our first instincts are always to avoid situations where telling the truth would hurt us. None of us likes pain.

"Look," he said, "what I'm talking about is not truth with a capital 'T.' And I really don't want to spend our time together arguing about moral values. Leave that to the theologians and philosophers. It's irrelevant to us, anyway.

"I repeat, truth has practical value to Good Communicators.

"Or, to put it another way, lies hurt Good Communicating. But I prefer the first definition. I want to put ideas with practical value to work for me," he said.

"So do I," the younger man said. "But I can see more pitfalls than practicality in this one."

"Certainly, there are pitfalls," the older man acknowledged. "And I grant you that the subject is complex. It certainly is—and should be—open to question and challenge. That's why it was important to have the Challenge Rule to lay the foundation.

"Let's take it back to the beginning of the process," he said. "You've considered your audience, even broken through your own ego barrier to do it. You've defined your message or messages and made sure that they hook the interest and meet the needs of your audience. You've challenged yourself and you think you can answer virtually any question presented to you.

"Say you've done all of that, but half of your message to your audience, half of your carefully constructed message, is built on lies or half truths. How do you think your audience will react?" the Good Communicator asked.

"With all that preparation, I think they'll accept the message," the younger man stated, with force.

"Not so," the Good Communicator said. "It would be much easier to manipulate your audience if it were, but your audience—one person or a multitude—can tell virtually every time that you're lying.

"And you're the one who tells them, with your body language. There are all kinds of physical signals. I suppose you could train yourself to avoid them all, but then you'd be so conscious of avoiding signals that you'd forget the message. In the long run, even in the short run, it's simply easier to tell the truth than to worry about controlling your body language. Leave that for actors and actresses of talent."

"I'm not sure everyone in my audience is sophisticated enough to read my body language well," the young man said.

"Perhaps not. But if they're listening to you, if they're paying attention, they will clearly get the feeling that something is out of sync, not quite right. They may even get that feeling from your logic, if it has holes in it and you ignore the holes. Your audience won't, believe me."

"I'm honestly not sure that I do," the young man said.

"I think this is going to be a long afternoon," the older man said with a sigh. "However, an understanding of the Truth Rule is essential to Good Communication, as essential as an understanding of the Audience Rule or any of the others. Without a genuine appreciation of the Truth Rule, you simply become a message manipulator.

"And there are countless thousands of message manipulators in the world. In whatever profession, message manipulators are people with the technical skills to be Good Communicators, but who haven't learned or who don't practice the Truth Rule...and by doing so start forgetting the Audience Rule, too.

"Let me pose a communications problem," he continued. "You are making a presentation to a small group of employees, and you have three points to make. The first is that the company is regretfully closing down operations at their location. The second is that they will all be transferred without change of status or pay to the other locations. The third is that you, personally, disagree with the decision and are sorry to be the bearer of sad tidings.

"The employees are not surprised to hear that their office is closing. There are very few real corporate secrets. From your body language, they clearly see that you are evading the issue and that your greatest desire is to leave the room quickly. Furthermore, they've seen you in meetings where they know the issue was discussed, and you were laughing with other executives.

"The fact is they don't believe your third point...the point where you said you personally disagreed with the decision and are sorry to announce it. What they do believe is that you were part of the decision and are simply sorry that the chore of announcing it fell on your shoulders.

"What do you suppose that does to your credibility on the other two points?" the older man asked.

The younger man sat silently.

"We both know that it destroys it," the Good Communicator said. "Your employees left that meeting believing that management didn't care about closing their office, and that there was substantial reason to doubt whether they'd get good placements at other offices...all because you prevaricated just a little to protect yourself from their anger.

"That little scenario may have only cost you bad feelings...unnecessary bad feelings. But perhaps one or more of those employees never got over their bad feelings about what management had callously done to them, perhaps they never believed that they would have new jobs, and they filed a lawsuit for wrongful termination. The company won it, $100,000 in legal fees later.

"Lies have a high cost in credibility. Sometimes the cost is in dollars, as well."

"I'm not convinced," the younger man said. "Sometimes withholding the truth, or sugarcoating it, is the kindest thing to do."

"It only seems that way," the older man said. "Sometimes a sugar pill helps us save face at the moment because it helps us avoid dealing with someone else's feelings.

"But in the long run, people don't remember your good intentions, your desire to protect them. What they remember is that you lied to them, or that you withheld information they thought was important.

"The result is that they won't hear anything else that you have to say on the subject, and probably on any other subject either.

"Let's work with another hypothetical situation," the older man continued. "Put yourself in the audience, say in a classroom. The professor lecturing at the front has just described an important concept in your field and gotten it dead wrong. Are you now going to believe his other statements without scepticism?"

The younger man shook his head negatively.

"Maybe the professor just made a mistake," the older man said. "But it undermined his credibility, his ability to be taken seriously by his audience. Now, suppose that he did it deliberately, and you somehow discovered that. How would you then react to the rest of his information?"

"I wouldn't believe any of it, or I'd check it all out for myself...if I had the time," the younger man admitted. "He just wouldn't have any credibility any more."

"Precisely," said the Good Communicator. "His facts became either irrelevant or questionable the instant his credibility went down the drain. That's important to remember.

"Now let's say this same professor was known to you and others for always being straightforward. And in the same class you got the same misinformation. What would your reaction be then?"

"I'd assume that he made a mistake, but that it wasn't by intent," the younger man said.

"But you would still trust him for other information, wouldn't you?" the older man asked. "Being human, you'd probably keep your ears open for other mistakes. But eventually you'd stop even doing that.

"What we're talking about is the fact that your credibility—your reputation for telling the truth consistently—is critically important to the way your audience receives your message. You may get a pass once from an audience that knows you, but twice or three times is unlikely. The more lies you tell, the less believable your true statements become. Eventually your audience finds it impossible to sort out your lies and the truth and gives up on you altogether.

"The fact is, even the truth is not believed when it comes from someone who is perceived to be a liar.

"Surely you've seen that happen to politicians frequently.

"Establishing your credibility by telling the truth is even more important when you've just met someone and you don't have a track record with them," the older man continued. "You rarely get a second chance with a new audience or a new acquaintance.

"I would go so far as to say that your credibility is infinitely more important than any fact or opinion you want to present," the Good Communicator continued. "Your ability to have your facts and opinions believed depends on how people perceive *you*."

"What happens when the facts change?" the younger man asked. "What happens when through no fault of mine, the information changes?"

"My experience has been that the audience will recall your past honesty," the older man said, "and will accept that the facts have changed. But if you have a reputation for dissemblance, they will believe that you withheld the truth the first time, and will act accordingly. Usually that means act with anger.

"Let's say that you're a CEO and you told employees in June that year-end earnings looked good and that they could all anticipate bonuses. But an unforeseen environmental disaster in November wiped out the increase, and you have to go back to your employees and tell them that there won't be any bonuses.

"If you're a CEO with credibility, your employees will be disappointed at the loss of income, but will accept what you have to say...partly because, if you're a Good Communicator, you discussed the disaster with them. But if you don't have credibility, they're likely to say that the disaster was a cop-out, an excuse not to pay them and to fatten the company coffers at their expense. Employee morale suffers, and turnover rises...all because the CEO didn't pay attention to the long-term impact of his personal credibility."

"Isn't it possible," the young man asked, "that no one would ever challenge the CEO and his information?"

"I can see that you're still trying to make a case for withholding information," the older man said.

The younger man nodded affirmatively.

"Is it possible that no one will ever challenge the authority of the speaker? I think not," the Good Communicator said, "although it is not only possible but probable that they won't do it to his face if he lacks credibility.

"We've all learned a lot from journalism these last two decades," he said. "Watergate taught us that there are no 'off limits' authorities, or 'off limits' questions, for that matter. Every authority is questioned. Competitive television broadcasting has brought us instant experience in our own living rooms, nightly challenges to the voices of authority, reinforcing the lessons of Watergate...and teaching us all how to be questioners on our own.

"There are far more reporters in the world than there used to be, and they are far more prepared and knowledgeable. Put that together with an increased propensity on all of our parts to question authority and I think you'll find very few situations, either public or private, that aren't intensely dissected and challenged. The odds of a misstatement or an outright lie going undetected or unchallenged get smaller every day."

The younger man groaned.

"There is in fact a simple and rather good test of the veracity and astuteness of your statements and decisions," the Good Communicator said.

The younger man looked up eagerly. "At this point, I'd welcome some simplicity. The road to your truth appears relentless."

"Yes," the older man chuckled, "I suppose it does. But that's only because it makes such strong business sense...personal, too.

"Here's the test: Can your statement or action hold up to challenge on *60 Minutes*? If it can, you're not only communicating, you're communicating with a clear conscience.

"I call it the Television Test," he said, laughing.

The younger man had a look of sheer incredulity on his face.

"Good lord," he said. "I don't want to make myself out as a liar, because I'm not. But it still seems to me that we're dealing with absolutes in situations where absolutes may not be necessary.

"For example," he said, "suppose I was talking to a group of employees about company growth. I talked to them about programs in place, what the future of the company looked like. But I didn't tell them about incomplete research in process that would substantially change the direction of the company and its market. I'd say that they didn't need to know. Would you say that the Truth Rule applies?"

"What do you think?" the older man answered. "What would a Good Communicator do? Of course I'd tell the truth.

"But I'd be honest enough to say that I couldn't discuss it in detail because the research wasn't done and the results weren't clear and the company was being careful about leaking potential competitive information until plans were solid.

"Essentially, I'd tell my audience that I *respected* their intelligence and their personal stake in the project but that I couldn't provide more details for any number of legitimate reasons. The audience is adult enough to deal with the truth. I want to show them that I respect their capabilities."

"I'm getting confused," the younger man said. "First you teil me to follow the Truth Rule without exception, and then you tell me not to tell my audience something."

"I think I see your problem," the older man said. "There are legitimate reasons not to give your audience information...but not respecting their capacity to deal with the information isn't one of them.

"At the very least, you owe them the respect of an honest explanation on why you can't give them information, or all of the information."

"So there *are* some legitimate reasons not to provide information," the younger man said. "What are they?"

"Let me think about them," the Good Communicator said. "Here are some business reasons not to provide information—I'm sure you can think of others:

..."The information would make the company lose a competitive advantage.

...The idea or product is being developed and is subject to much change or revision before it is finished.

...Lawsuits have been filed and statements might prejudice the outcome of the suits.

...The information is highly technical—remember the Language Rule—and would require a strong technical or professional background to put in proper perspective.

...Releasing the information at this time would prejudice additional activity or negotiations now in progress or under consideration.

...Key parties must be notified before the data can be released.

...Release of the information to a select group would violate laws or regulations, particularly securities regulations.

...The information requested is of a personal nature and is not an appropriate topic for a larger audience.

...You may not have the information.

...You've been asked not to discuss it. "

"The point is," the older man said, "that you owe your audience an honest assessment of why you can't be totally open with them. Then you don't lose your all-important credibility. And you demonstrate that you respect your audience's capabilities and intelligence...another way of telling them that they're important to you.

"Those are good reasons for not providing information," the young man acknowledged. "But what about
not providing information in personal relationships?
I just can't see how the same rules apply."

"Well, it's certainly much more complex," the older
man laughed. "And interpersonal 'truth' is certainly
an area where we could get seduced into talking about
moral and ethical issues, and even psychological
ones. Since neither one of us is a psychologist nor a
philosopher, I think we ought to stick to pragmatic
uses of 'truth' in talking about interpersonal
relationships.

"It seems to me," he said, "that what happens when
we decide we like someone—or decide that we've
fallen in love with someone—is that we adopt a view
of that other person consistent with their view of
themselves. We think "Oh, that's a neat person and I
want to get to know them better."

The young man nodded his agreement.

"The process of doing that...of getting to know them
better...is one of uncovering truths about them," the
Good Communicator said. "That's pretty basic,
wouldn't you agree?"

The young man nodded again.

"So truth serves a totally practical purpose in helping
people get to know each other. That's assuming, of
course, that their goal really is to get to know each
other.

"Removing the truth from the relationship means
that the process of knowledge stops. So from a practical viewpoint, if you decide to stop telling the truth,
or you decide to hedge on it a little, you've stopped

the process of letting the other person know you. I can't tell you whether that's the right or wrong thing to do in the circumstances. But I can tell you that that's what happens. Lies, or half-truths, or withholding information simply stop a relationship from growing because the knowledge process stops. You have to decide whether that's the result you want or can accept.

"Lying—or just not telling the truth—has another long-term effect on interpersonal relationships," the older man continued. "That has to do with credibility. We were talking about it a minute ago in terms of more impersonal audiences.

"When you lose credibility with someone who likes you, someone who has accepted much of your vision of yourself, you are changing the nature of the relationship. You are not seen as the same person. You may continue to have the same image of yourself but the other person no longer does. They may decide, as a result, that they no longer want to maintain the relationship as it is.

"People decide to stay in personal relationships for any number of reasons, but when the credibility goes, much of the glue often goes with it," the Good Communicator said. "I think the need to tell the truth and thus to maintain credibility is as important and practical in personal relationships as it is with larger audiences.

"Telling the truth...maintaining your credibility...is probably the toughest rule to follow," the Good Communicator said. "And that's not only because we're predisposed to hide information to make life easier. It's also because our audiences scrutinize so much of what we say."

"I'm getting confused again," the young man said. "I thought we were talking about truth and credibility, and you keep going back to talking about the audience."

"Why, yes, that's true," said the Good Communicator. "Part of the reason we have so much trouble maintaining credibility—and why integrity is so important—is that audiences are so amazingly bright.

"That's true whether the audience is one person or a group. As speakers, as communicators, we frequently make the deadly mistake of underestimating the intelligence of our audience and its capacity to understand. That impacts our willingness to present the truth.

"We're so sure that we have a lock on the truth, on the completeness of the information, on our own opinions...particularly if we use the Challenge Rule effectively...that we can't imagine the audience may not accept what we have to say. Remember, we talked about the need to hook the interest of the audience earlier."

The young man nodded, remembering.

"Now we're talking about the audience and its capacity to hear, understand, or discern the truth...and how well the audience accepts your message after they've filtered it.

"Bad communicators always tend to underestimate the ability of the audience to discern the truth," the Good Communicator said. "They even assume that the audience won't recognize the truth unless it is specifically pronounced.

"It's a classic mistake," the older man continued. "It happens all the time in business, and in our personal lives, too. We may be providing our audience with a thousand clues as to what is really going on, but since we don't *tell* them—since we don't use the words directly—we truly think they don't know.

"That's fundamentally naive, of course, but it seems to be one large area where businesspeople are enormously naive and blind.

"They forget that truth is truth and fact is fact, even if the words don't come from their own mouths. And the audience is normally quite capable of discerning the truth without hearing the magic words from on high, wherever on high is. Yet would-be communicators continue to delude themselves that the people around them don't know the truth, just because no statement has been made...or that they won't recognize the facts when someone stands in front of them and denies them."

"I guess Lincoln knew what he was talking about," the younger man said, "when he said 'you can fool all the people some of the time and some of the people all the time, but you cannot fool all the people all of the time.'"

"Yes," said the older man, laughing. "Did you know that same quote is sometimes attributed to P. T. Barnum? And if a 19th century politician and a 19th century showman didn't believe you could fool the public, what makes you think—living in the age of high intensity journalism and television—that you can?

"All right, all right. I believe," said the younger man. "I might as well tell the truth."

The Truth Rule:

You might as well tell it.

• Credibility is the most important thing you have to sell. It is more important than fact.

• Your listener can almost always tell whether or not you're lying.

• If your listener believes you're lying, there is no possibility that what you have to say will be heard.

• If your listener believes you're lying on one subject, he's likely to disregard what you have to say on other subjects.

• If you maintain your credibility, people will believe you when the facts change.

• There are so many people concerned with gathering information as a career that the chances are slim that your lie will escape undetected in a public arena.

• Your audience is grown up enough to deal with the truth. Respect their capabilities.

• We delude ourselves by thinking that people can't see the truth unless we tell it to them, or when we tell them it doesn't exist.

The Bad News Rule

"I GUESS part of what disturbs me with the Truth Rule," the young man said at the next meeting, "is its potential to create a real flap.

"The last thing in the world I want to do is end up with a front page headline quoting me on something negative. Why in the world do reporters go after the bad news, anyway?"

"What we call bad news is events that are out of the ordinary," the older man responded. "We expect things to go right most of the time.

"We expect businesses to make a profit. We expect traffic to flow smoothly. We expect our neighbors to act peaceably. We expect government to be honest and relatively effective. We expect the weather to be moderate, in season.

"No one," he said, "sits down in the cafeteria with their co-workers and enumerates all the things that went smoothly and predictably today. It's simply too boring to imagine."

"That's true," said the younger man. "But why do people get so excited about bad news? Why do reporters, especially, get excited about bad news?"

"Don't underestimate the pure excitement value of bad or uncommon news. We all want a little excitement in our lives," the Good Communicator said. "Bad news is exciting, just like racy gossip. In fact, the only thing the two don't have in common is the subject matter...and sometimes they have that, too."

"Don't reporters understand that they're hurting people with bad news?" the young man asked. "Don't they realize they're doing damage?"

"I'm sure that they do, some of the time," the older man said. "But they also have to balance the potential damage, real or imagined, against the public's right to know or interest in knowing. That's a fine line, I know, and when we're the person the bad news concerns, we probably feel that they tip the scales the wrong direction."

The young man nodded vigorously.

"It always helps me to remember that the headline on the front page can never be too big when I've done something I want the world to know about, and it can't be too small or too far back in the paper when I've done something I'd rather no one knew," the Good Communicator said. "Our all-important egos trick us into thinking that our personal feelings are consistent with good news judgment."

The young man laughed.

"Reporters have to walk a line serving what they perceive to be the best interests of the community at large," the older man continued. "If we're the people involved, we tend to believe that they're always on the wrong side of that line. Sometimes they are, of course. They're no more perfect than the rest of us.

"When I'm the subject of the news, I try to remember that the reporter's job isn't pleasing me," he said. "In fact—and by now I'm sure this won't surprise you—I look at it as my job to follow the rules of Good Communicating and bring the reporter around to my viewpoint, if that's possible."

"No, that isn't a surprise," the younger man said. "Not anymore. But I still don't understand why everyone seems to get such a charge out of bad news."

"I think that's because bad news has market value," the older man responded. "We can do something with it. It calls for a response on some level. Sometimes that level is financial.

"Sometimes it's moral, and sometimes it's simply psychological. But we react to it."

"I need an example," the young man said.

"All right. Let's go back to the example of a plant closing," the Good Communicator said. "We can all agree that the news is sad.

"Some people in the town would simply shake their heads in sorrow and feel bad for those who had lost their jobs. They might even feel nostalgic for the days when the plant was a vibrant part of the community.

"Stockbrokers would assess the closing from the perspective of both the long-term and short-term financial health of the company and would make recommendations to their clients based on that assessment.

"The family down the street might call a real estate agent and put their house on the market because they knew that they would have to leave town to support themselves.

"Union leaders would be calling a meeting to determine what steps they could take to protect jobs and income.

"Community leaders would be busy figuring out what they could do to keep the plant or replace it, so that the community would continue to be economically healthy.

"Retailers at the local mall would be figuring out what they needed to do to reduce inventories and labor costs.

"Attorneys might be planning how to file lawsuits on behalf of employees who are losing their jobs.

"Legislators might be figuring out what they can do to protect communities from sudden economic dislocations like plant closings.

"And all the workers at the plant across the street might be very grateful that it wasn't them.

"In other words," the older man said, "the information has value to the marketplace, even if it's just to elicit an emotional response."

"But good news has market value, too," the younger man said. "Why don't people get as excited about good news?"

"I think it's because the range is so much more limited...and we can talk about that another time," the Good Communicator answered. "Bad news is relevant to more of us most of the time. For example, an airline crash might cause us to rethink our travel plans. We take a safe landing for granted. A celebrity's divorce is great gossip at a dinner party, but the Jones's divorce probably isn't. Some bad news we pay attention to just because it makes us feel superior to the rest of the human race."

"Well, all things considered, I'd still rather keep bad news quiet," the young man said.

"One of the problems with bad news," the older man said with a laugh, "is that it very seldom stays quiet. If you think about it, that's understandable. Remember Ben Franklin's line... 'Three may keep a secret if two of them are dead?'

"As long as one other person knows, the odds are extremely high that more than one other person will eventually know. And the news will continue to spread. And remember the sophistication of the people asking the questions and demanding truthful answers these days...whether they're our friends, colleagues or professional reporters.

"Your ability to keep bad news buried is dreadfully limited these days," the Good Communicator continued. "And, of course, if you're following the Truth Rule, you'd be very concerned about the loss of your credibility when the bad news finally comes out, as it generally does."

"Honestly, all I want to do is make the bad news go away," the young man said.

"You're not alone," the older man responded. "That's what everyone wants to do with bad news...make it go away.

"Well, it goes away faster if you're the one who announces it."

"That doesn't make sense to me," the younger man said. "Why would it go away faster?"

"When you wait until the gossip reaches critical mass, or until the reporter calls, you've given lots of people lots of time to speculate about what's really going on and why no one is talking about it. It must really be awful if no one will talk about it, right?" the older man asked.

"By the time the actual news is heard, all of that speculation about the news itself and the fact that no one will discuss it has escalated until you have a major brouhaha, and people are unlikely to believe that what you say is the whole story or the truthful story," he continued.

"If you get the news out right away, it has more limited excitement value. All the information is available and there's simply a limit to how long people are willing to discuss it.

"The faster you get it out, the faster the discussion stops and the less fuel there is to feed it. Journalists frequently remind themselves that today's headline ends up on the bottom of a birdcage tomorrow. There's nothing older than yesterday's news. Today's gossip has a much longer lifespan.

"Bad news is still bad news," the Good Communicator said. "We shouldn't forget that. But you reduce its importance by dealing with it quickly. And you get to maintain your credibility by announcing it yourself.

"People really get mad...personally mad...when you're the person they're supposed to get the news from and they're getting it somewhere else. Then you really lose credibility because they think you're evading the issue. And they'd be right."

The young man groaned. "I feel like I'm slowly being squeezed by these arguments. But the truth is, I really would like to evade the issue."

"The truth is, we all would," the older man said. "But the fact is that in virtually every case, doing that hurts us in the long run through loss of credibility. It hurts us in the short run, too, because we invite specu- lation and gossip based on faulty information. And evading the issue keeps it alive longer.

"Saying 'no comment' usually makes people think you're hiding something," he continued. "And they're usually right. Otherwise, you'd just answer the question. There are times when you can't answer the question, and have very good reasons for it. In those cases, you simply give the reason. I think we talked about some of those reasons before."

"It's too bad there isn't a way to say 'no comment' in a personal relationship," the young man said. "There are lots of times when I'd like to do that."

"I'll bet that you've found a way to do that," the Good Communicator said. "I'll bet that you say 'I don't want to talk about it.'"

The young man laughed.

"It has the same effect as 'no comment' in a public situation," the older man said. "The other person thinks, usually rightfully, that you're hiding something. You lose credibility, and you lose your opportunity to control the message you're ultimately going to have to deliver.

"Trying to evade delivering bad news—or trying to disguise it as good news—is just another way of trying to hide from reality. Reality usually wins anyhow, and you pay the price for it."

The Bad News Rule:

Bad news has market value.

• The headline can never be too small when we've done something we'd rather no one knew. It can't be too big when we're proud of ourselves.

• Bad news is exciting because it has market value. Lawyers can file cases. Brokers can trade stocks. Neighbors can count themselves lucky that it didn't happen to them.

• Bad news is almost always more exciting than good news because it has relevancy to more people.

• Bad news almost always comes out.

• Bad news always goes away faster if you announce it.

• You make people really mad when they get the bad news from someone else.

• No comment makes people think you're hiding something. Usually they're right. "I don't want to talk about it" is the way we usually say "no comment" to people close to us.

• Trying to tell people bad news is really good news makes them wonder whether you're crazy or they are.

The Good News Rule

"I HAVE AN equal amount of trouble," the young man said, "figuring out why reporters aren't interested in good news."

"Sometimes they are," the Good Communicator said. "But good news, for the most part, doesn't have the same draw that bad news does. Oh, there are exceptions. A good news event of enormous scope would be one of them...like a nationwide charity event. Good news on the sports pages always gets attention, but one person's good news in sports is always someone else's bad news.

"An awful lot of good news just isn't very exciting. And there isn't very much you can do with it. Unlike bad news, it doesn't have much 'market value.' There are exceptions to that, too...I especially think of investment decisions...but generally good news doesn't generate the same kind of activity.

"You just don't get a front page headline when traffic is flowing smoothly. I'd bet that if the federal budget ever balances, no one will pay much attention after the first couple of years. We'll take it for granted, like we do most good news."

"I'd bet that it gets buried on the back pages of the newspaper and never gets mentioned more than one day," the young man said.

"I'd bet you're right," the older man laughed. "That's one of the problems with good news.

"Good news doesn't last long.

"And since it has limited market value," the Good Communicator continued, "there isn't much of an incentive for following up on the story. Even more often, there isn't much of a story to follow up on. What do you say after the company announces good earnings? That, after all, is what it's supposed to do.

"What do you say after you say 'congratulations' to a wedding announcement?

"And after the lottery winner is announced, there isn't any more news until he's gotten used to having money. Even then, there isn't much of a story in someone's having good fortune."

"Every time I read about someone winning the lottery, my strongest feeling is regret that it isn't me," the young man said.

"That's another reason good news doesn't get the attention that bad news does," the older man said. "When it happens to someone else, it makes us envious...if we acknowledge our all-too-human feelings. It makes us just the smallest bit wistful about the fact that it isn't happening to us. Bad news may make us do something in reaction. But good news— usually—just makes us feel something in reaction.

"And unless we have a personal investment in the good news event...in which case it's obviously wonderful beyond its true possible scope...what it usually makes us feel is just the littlest bit jealous.

"The headlines for our own good news can't be big enough, or far enough forward in the newspaper, or the story can't possibly get enough time on the evening news if it's our good news. Our friends can't possibly celebrate wildly enough, or long enough...for us.

"But the reverse is true, too. They can't possibly forget fast enough if it's bad news.

"Good news always engenders the strongest and the only lingering feelings in those people it affects directly. The further away you get from direct impact, the less significant good news becomes.

"It makes people question the quality of their own lives. They may be relieved not to have bad news, but they'll be discomfited by not having good news.

"That's one of the primary reasons good news has such a limited life span," the Good Communicator said. "It makes people examine their own lives, and most of us would prefer not to have to do that.

"In fact, the only people I know who can deal with good news routinely and comfortably all of the time are those people who already have lots of it...and I don't think there are many of them," he said.

"The Good News and Bad News Rules are just ways of giving us new perspectives. *They help us understand why our unique concerns aren't shared by everyone around us*. The news is never as good nor as bad to someone else as it is to us.

"Well. I think we've finished," the Good Communicator said. "Those are the rules. There are boundless techniques to help you implement them, but you probably don't need them unless you intend to become a professional communicator."

"I've certainly learned a lot, and I've certainly disagreed with a lot," the younger man said. "Gradually I've come to understand your perspective and to be able to apply it to my own life...which, incidentally, is going much more smoothly."

"I'm very glad to hear that," the older man said. "This is certainly an instance of good news that I'm very pleased to hear."

"I do have one more question," the younger man said. "I understand the rules, and I'm beginning to be able to use them. I'm even developing some of my own techniques. But what is a Good Communicator?"

The Good News Rule:

Good news doesn't last long.

• Good news isn't very exciting. It's more exciting if you can make a profit on it.

• Good news is only wonderful to those people who have a vested interest in it.

• Good news makes other people not so sure of their own lives. They sweep it away so they don't have to question their own lives.

• The only people who can deal with good news routinely are those who already have lots of it.

Good Communicating

"THE EASY answer is that a Good Communicator is a person who understands and follows all of the rules," the Good Communicator answered. "And that's true. But it's too easy.

"Better to say that a Good Communicator is a person who respects the people he or she is communicating with, and who makes a diligent effort to reach the other person and share knowledge and perspective.

"A Good Communicator is also a person who understands and accepts the occasions when the other person can't or won't be reached," he said.

"Conversely, a bad communicator is a person who continually underestimates either the intelligence or the concerns of his or her audience, and who keeps beating the audience over the head with his message even when the audience has clearly demonstrated a lack of interest or belief.

"And sometimes," he laughed, "being a Good Communicator is knowing when to stop."